BOOK ANALYSIS

Written by Dominique Coutant-Defer
Translated by Jessica Foster

AF126400

The Sorrows of
Young Werther

BY JOHANN WOLFGANG VON GOETHE

GOETHE

GERMAN WRITER

- **Born in Frankfurt in 1749**
- **Died in Weimar in 1832**
- **Notable works:**
  - *The Sorrows of Young Werther* (1774), novel
  - *Wilhelm Meister's Apprenticeship* (1795-1796), novel
  - *Faust* (1808-1832), play

Born in Frankfurt in 1749, the writer Johann Wolfgang von Goethe is considered to be the precursor to the European Romanticism movement. Coming from a wealthy, middle-class background, he studied to become a lawyer at the Imperial Court of Justice. But very early on, writing became his passion and his vast corpus, made up of plays, poems and novels, placed Germany at the forefront of the literary scene for half a century. Goethe was passionate about music, and met Mozart and Beethoven. Science also interested him and he wrote a treatise on colours and works on natural history. His two masterpieces, *Faust* (1808-1832) and *The Sorrows of Young Werther* (1774), are famous throughout the world.

THE SORROWS OF YOUNG WERTHER

A MASTERPIECE OF THE ROMANTIC ERA

- **Genre:** epistolary novel
- **Reference edition:** Goethe, J. W. (2012) *The Sorrows of Young Werther*. Trans. Boylan, R. D. USA: Renaissance Classics.
- **First edition:** 1774
- **Themes:** love, despair, suicide, sensitivity, nature

Published in 1774, the epistolary novel *The Sorrows of Young Werther* was one of Goethe's first works. This tragic story describes the all-consuming passion of Werther, a sensitive and excited young man, for young Charlotte, in whom he thinks he has found his soulmate, but who is engaged to another man. The young man tries to leave her, but comes back to her and is gradually consumed by this impossible love. This novel, which sets out the basis for Romanticism, was extremely successful.

SUMMARY

BOOK I

The first letters from Werther to his friend Wilhelm date from May 1771. He writes about the joy of having left the city, where amazing prospects awaited him, and having found a "terrestrial paradise" (p. 3), Walheim, where he takes great pleasure in his solitude and his long walks in the mountains, feeling a divine presence everywhere. He describes the little village that he goes down to sometimes and the local people he has befriended despite their natural savagery. He refuses to let his friend send him books; "his Homer" is sufficient. He states that, in any case, human life is fanciful and that only nature, with its inexhaustible riches, inspires artists. He often describes what is before his eyes.

In mid-June he writes that, during a country dance, he has met Charlotte, the daughter of the district judge, who is engaged to Albert, a young man from a good family who is currently away on business. He saw her for the first time as she was handing out slices of bread to her six brothers and sisters who seem to adore her. "[M]y whole soul was absorbed by her air, her voice, her manner" (p. 11), writes Werther, captivated by her dark eyes. The young people discover that they have the same fondness for lyrical poetry.

From July onwards, he often goes to visit her and bonds with the children, in whom he sees the seed of all virtue. Moreover, the generosity of Charlotte, who visits all the sick people in the region, moves him deeply. He is soon convinced that he loves her, despite the love she seems to have for her fiancé. She becomes almost sacred to him and every day without her torments him. He draws her outline in the same way as a shadow puppet. Unfortunately, Albert returns. Werther finds him commendable: he compares his calm temperament to his own, which is rather excitable and worried, and realises that he must give up on Charlotte.

In August, Wilhelm advises him to try to seduce Charlotte or to leave. But the young man is undecided and says that he is going crazy. He borrows some guns from Albert for a walk in the mountains and, as a joke, holds one up to his head, knowing that it is not loaded. Albert then tells him his disapproval of suicide, which he considers to be a weakness, and Werther replies that he must distinguish the motives from the action.

He often goes from elation to despondency, and complains about his excessive sensitivity. On his birthday, he receives from Charlotte something he had often asked her for: a pink ribbon from the dress she was wearing when they first met. "What is to come of all this wild, aimless, endless passion?" (p. 31), he wonders.

In September, he decides to take a job in an embassy, without telling anyone. He befriends Miss B., whose charming company he enjoys.

BOOK II

He does not like life at the embassy and pours his heart out in long letters to Charlotte, who tells him that she has got married. Werther had promised to get rid of his paper silhouette of Charlotte on her wedding day. Once that date has passed however, he keeps it.

In March he resigns following an altercation with the ambassador, who had made it clear to him that the place of a commoner was not in the court.

In May he sets off on a journey to his hometown, and stays with an aristocrat. But he gets bored and, in the end, admits: "I wish to be near Charlotte again, that is all" (p. 44).

In July he rebels against God as he has not joined him to Charlotte who is, he believes, not right for Albert. Albert's death would fix things, he thinks.

In August, he goes back to Walheim. He meets a young farmhand and sympathises with him: he was fired because he was in love with the farmer's wife. He regretfully gets rid of the worn-out clothes he was wearing the first time he danced with Charlotte. He starts going to her house again, and becomes irritated by all her adorable mannerisms, which reawaken his desire. He does not understand how Albert does not seem as happy as he ought to.

In autumn he gives up on reading Homer to read Ossian (legendary Scottish hero and bard of the 3rd century), whose tormented elation he enjoys, and complains of having a large amount of undeveloped love within him. "Heaven, how often I lie down in my bed with a wish, and even a hope, that I may never awaken again," writes Werther (p. 50). Charlotte reproaches him for his excesses and his impassioned declarations, but she is aware of his extreme sorrow.

During a conversation with a poor man in the countryside, he learns that the latter was only happy when he was shut in a mental asylum. Werther almost begins to envy this man who has lost his mind. He learns that this "happy mortal" (p. 53) was secretary to Charlotte's father who fired him because he had fallen in love with the young girl.

On 4 December, when he begs Charlotte to stop playing a tune on the piano that upsets him, the young woman asks him to leave, believing him to be ill.

The letters to Wilhelm stop after this date and the editor claims that the rest of the book is composed of witness accounts collected from those who were close to Werther and of information from papers found at his house.

Werther is increasingly unhappy and his mind is deteriorating. He becomes unfair towards Albert, who he thinks has become distant from Charlotte and, at the same time, accuses himself of disrupting their marriage. He learns that the farmhand who had previously been sacked from the farm where he worked has just killed his replacement. Werther pleads his case before the district judge in vain. Albert asks Charlotte to distance herself from the young man, whose incessant visits have started to stir gossip. "[H] is powers became exhausted without aim or design, until they brought him to a sorrowful end" (p. 58).

In December a thaw floods the vale of Walheim, and in despair the young man contemplates the unrecognisable places of his old walks with Charlotte. A letter addressed to Wilhelm, dated 20 December, is found at Werther's house: it states his irrevocable decision to end his life. Another letter to Charlotte the following day talks of the same plan, reaffirming his violent passion for her. He goes to her in the evening and she asks him to read her his translation of Ossian's songs. Charlotte is upset when he reads them, and falls passionately into his arms. That is the last time they see each other. He bids her farewell and leaves the house. The next day, he sends his servant to borrow Albert's guns, which he claims to want to take on his travels. Albert asks Charlotte, who is very shaken by the events of the night before, to fetch them. When he learns that she touched the weapons, Werther writes to the young woman that he is happy to die by her hands.

His servant finds him the next morning, dying from a bullet that he shot into his head. Charlotte faints when she hears the news. Albert and the whole family of the district judge gather round the wounded man, whom the doctor tries in vain to save. He dies at midday. He is buried at night, without any clergy present, while we fear for Charlotte's life.

CHARACTER STUDY

WERTHER

This young man, who is never described physically, left his hometown to move to Walheim. He has a solitary and sensitive temperament, is close to nature and pours out his feelings in long, lyrical letters written to his friend Wilhelm, in which he describes his admiration for the landscapes and the simple and rustic ways of the villagers. His friend will also, in the first part of the work, be his confidant when he speaks of his ardent passion for Charlotte, whom he met at a country ball. Werther thinks that he will be able to forget this impossible love by leaving Walheim and striking up a relationship with another young girl. But he is irresistibly drawn to Charlotte and the young man, rebelling against God and fate who perpetually deny him this young woman, who is married to another, can find no way out other than suicide.

CHARLOTTE

Werther is immediately seduced by this young girl with dark eyes, "of middle height, with a lovely figure, dressed in a robe of simple white, trimmed with pink ribbons" (p. 11), when he meets her at the start of the novel. "I found penetration and character in everything she said: every expression seemed to brighten her features with new charms" (p. 11), he continues. The daughter of the local district judge, with no mother, she raises her six brothers and sisters with love and devotion. She shares Werther's passion for lyrical poetry and music. She is deeply attracted to the young man, but she is engaged and later married to a man whom she respects and is very fond of, and therefore never gives into her love for Werther, whose elated excesses she seems to be somewhat afraid of.

ALBERT

Engaged and later married to Charlotte, Albert is a decent man, with strict moral values, who condemns suicide. Werther recognises his great qualities and the two men become friends. Although he detects Werther's passion for Charlotte, Albert never closes the door to him and looks after him while he is dying.

ANALYSIS

A literary form

Epistolary novels were one of the most common forms of novel in the 18th century. *Letters of a Portuguese Nun* by Guilleragues (French writer, 1628-1685), published in 1669, was a series of love letters purportedly written by a Portuguese nun, which were taken as a model for this genre. Montesquieu (French writer, 1689-1755) openly follows this example in his *Persian Letters* (1721). The success of Richardson's (English writer, 1689-1761) great novels (*Pamela: Or, Virtue Rewarded*; *Clarissa: Or the History of a Young Lady*) also increased the success of this genre and spread it around all European countries. The enthusiasm incited in 1782 by the publication of *Dangerous Liaisons* by Laclos (French writer, 1741-1803) is proof of this.

Writing about the self

Unlike the polyphonic style of writing in which several voices are often heard, through the means of letters written by different people, Goethe's novel practically only gives the floor to the main character, young Werther, which reinforces the value of subjectivity and private space that we find in the epistolary genre. Goethe claims that the end of the novel was written based on third party witnesses to the last weeks of the hero's life (his correspondence with Wilhelm having finished), but there is a lot of information obtained from letters that were never sent and later found among Werther's possessions after his death.

Epistolary narration is unique in that it does not describe external events or extravagant adventures, but only their effect on the letter-writer and their mood. The reader therefore gets the internal story of the characters, their character and their evolution, through the internal viewpoint that is necessarily adopted in this genre. The dramatic twists and unexpected developments are more psychological than factual. "[A] letter is the portrait of the soul; [...] it yields to all our actions by turns," says the Chevalier Danceny in *Dangerous Liasons*. Through writing, the letter-writer describes himself, especially as the letter is often contemporary to the events recounted. Thus, Werther warmly describes meeting Charlotte: "I have made an acquaintance who has won my heart" (p. 9), insisting that he is "a happy and contented mortal, but a poor historian" (p. 10), which highlights the purely subjective aspect of his narration of the events.

A LITERARY TREND: ROMANTICISM

The origins of Romanticism

Romanticism was a literary and cultural trend which came about at the end of the 18th century, firstly in Germany, then in England and France, which would soon conquer all of Europe in all the arts. The writer Richardson with his novel *Clarissa: Or the History of a Young Lady* (1747-1748), the English poet William Blake with his *Songs of Innocence* (1789), Jean-Jacques Rousseau (French writer, 1712-1778) with *Julie, or the New Heloise* (1761) and Goethe's publication of

The Sorrows of Young Werther all contributed to propagating this romantic ideal. Goethe was also one of the leading figures of the literary and political movement *Sturm und Drang* (which can be translated as 'storm and stress'), which was the starting point for Romanticism and which, in the absolutist Germany of the time, extols individual freedom whose nature is one of the most favoured settings and major themes of the Romantic period.

In 1760, the Scottish poet James Macpherson (1736-1796) published a collection of elegiac poems, attributed to a Scottish bard, Ossian, which was extremely successful. Goethe, additionally, has Werther and Charlotte read Ossian. The text's authenticity was, however, later contested and often considered as a mere invention by Macpherson. The foundations for Romanticism were nonetheless laid down, as a reaction against Classicism and the rationalism of the Enlightenment. The idea of interiority is strongly emphasised as well as the return to nature, as a source of inspiration for artists and as a place of refuge.

This literary trend lasted until the second half of the 19th century with writers such as Lamartine (French writer, 1790-1869), Chateaubriand (French writer, 1768-1848) and Hugo (French writer, 1802-1885) who, in the preface to his play *Cromwell*, written in 1827, signed the manifesto of French Romantic drama. Musset (French writer, 1810-1885), a little later, invented the expression 'mal du siècle' (which can be translated roughly as 'malady of the century'), to illustrate the Romantic hero's state of mind, helpless in the face of his dreams of freedom being restricted by social demands.

Romantic themes

- The emphasis on individuality: the Romantic hero does not perceive himself as an ordinary member of society. He instead leans towards isolation and solitude, as is the case with Werther. Moreover, this effect is emphasised in Goethe's novel due to the fact that the reader is not aware of his recipient Wilhelm's replies. The novel begins thus: "How happy I am that I am gone! My dear friend, what a thing is the heart of man! To leave you, from whom I have been inseparable, whom I love so dearly, and yet to feel happy!" (p. 2). In the same vein, Werther, during his stay at the embassy, harshly judges the worldly attitudes of the court and does not think twice about returning to solitude.

- The exaggeration of feelings: relative to the emphasis on people's individuality, they are essentially focused on themselves and their emotions. Romantic literature emphasises each man's own interiority, through heroes who lyrically express their excitement as much as their sorrows, which are often caused by dissatisfaction. Indeed, the Romantic hero, advocating a solitary life, is essentially frustrated by his contact with reality, whose obstacles he cannot manage. Thus, Werther clashes with Albert, who denies him Charlotte, cannot find his place at the embassy, etc. He is drawn to marginal beings (the madman he meets in the countryside, the murdering farmhand) and tempted by the same vices. Unable to integrate into reality, he goes through a phase of rebellion and falls victim to excesses which develop to a violent and exaggerated extent. We are far from the currently accepted meaning of the adjective 'romantic'. Werther is elated, verging on mad, and violently suffers from the frustration of his unsatisfied desire: "How my heart beats when by accident I touch her finger, or my feet meet hers under the table!" (p. 21), writes the young man, impassioned by love for this woman who belongs to another. He also dreams of Albert's death and feels even more distraught when he recognises his rival's many qualities. As wes can see, Romantic heroes live intensely and have necessarily intense emotions and all-consuming passions, such as that which draws Werther to Charlotte. Goethe's work therefore matches the culture of heightened sensitivity that characterises Romanticism. This sensitivity is seen as a positive attribute which draws the attention of the outside world. It also allows for communication between people without using language: Werther and Charlotte's enraptured contemplation of the countryside after the storm leaves them speechless, but they naturally take each other by the hand.

- Nature: nature appears in Romantic literature, on the one hand, as a source of inspiration for artists and writers (Rousseau or Lamartine, for example) or as a pretext for the main character to pour forth his sensitivity. On the other hand, it can be a significant, symbolic element of the narration. Indeed, the natural cycle of the seasons plays an important role in *The Sorrows of Young Werther*: it is no accident that the narrator's passion for Charlotte begins in spring, at the time of year in which the character is enraptured by the rebirth of nature ("A wonderful serenity has taken possession of my entire soul, like these sweet mornings of spring which I enjoy with my whole heart", p. 3). And autumn and winter of the following year are the setting for the protagonist's descent into hell and suicide. Nature is also linked to his devastated state of mind due to his impossible love, for example by offering him the sorry sight of the vale that is so dear to him, as it was the setting for his walks with Charlotte, being flooded by a sudden thaw. Conversely, it is also present in the euphoria of his first moments of love: the young friends share kind words beneath the moonlight.

The Sorrows of Young Werther, the first novel of an almost unknown author, aged 25, which was different from the thick novels of the time on account of its modest size, was immediately successful in Germany. Some literary journals, however, judged it immoral, seeing it as an endorsement of suicide. Additionally, some readers saw Werther as an example to follow and committed suicide. Several re-editions have been produced since 1775, and the first English translation was published in 1779, illustrating how famous the German text had already become.

FURTHER REFLECTION

SOME QUESTIONS TO THINK ABOUT...

- Having read *The Sorrows of Young Werther*, do you think that the meaning we often give to the adjective 'romantic' is appropriate?
- What role does nature play in Goethe's text? Is it more than just a setting for the action?
- Goethe's novel is an epistolary novel: how does the author's choice of genre reinforce the subjective character of the work?
- Summarise the main stages of Werther's passion for Charlotte. Give details and titles for each one.
- Werther's suicide is, in a way, foreshadowed from the beginning of the story. At what points in the text is it most noticeable?
- What relationships does the main character have with others when he escapes his solitude?
- Charlotte, the main female character of the novel, does not only have a romantic dimension. What other aspects of her personality are attractive to Werther?
- Albert is Werther's rival. What kind of relationship do the two men have? What do you think about this?

We want to hear from you!
Leave a comment on your online library
and share your favourite books on social media!

FURTHER READING

REFERENCE EDITION

- Goethe, J. W. (2012) *The Sorrows of Young Werther.* Trans. Boylan, R. D. USA: Renaissance Classics.

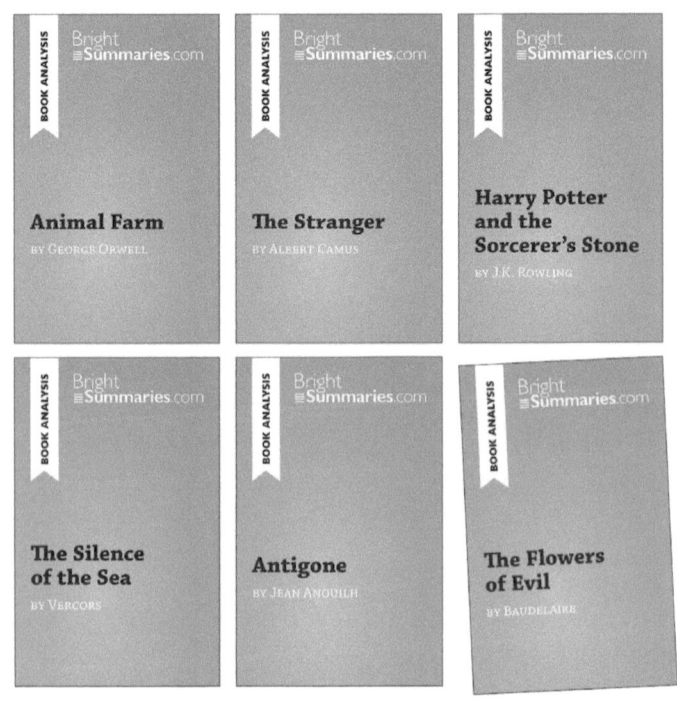